#39400

D0515831

Siskiyou County
School Library

SCIENCE IN ACTION
Air, Air Everywhere

By Tom Johnston
Illustrated by Sarah Pooley

39400

Gareth Stevens Publishing
Milwaukee

39400

Library of Congress Cataloging-in-Publication Data

Johnston, Tom.
  Air, air everywhere.

  (Science in action)
  British ed. published under title: Let's imagine, air. c1985.
  Includes index.
  Summary: Illustrates the properties of air, how air works for us, and how we use and abuse it.
  1. Air--Juvenile literature. (1. Air) I. Pooley, Sarah, ill. II. Title.
III. Series: Science in action (Milwaukee, Wis.)
QC161.2.J64 1988   551.5   87-42752
ISBN 1-55532-431-2
ISBN 1-55532-406-1 (lib. bdg.)

North American edition first published in 1988 by

Gareth Stevens, Inc.   7317 West Green Tree Road
Milwaukee, Wisconsin 53223, USA

This US edition copyright © 1988. First published as *Let's Imagine: Air* in the United Kingdom by
The Bodley Head, London.

Text copyright © 1985 Tom Johnston.
Illustrations copyright © 1985 Sarah Pooley.

All rights reserved. No part of this book may be reproduced or utilized in any form or by any means
without permission in writing from Gareth Stevens, Inc.

Hand lettering: Kathy Hall.
Typeset by Web Tech, Milwaukee.
Project editor: MaryLee Knowlton.

Technical consultants: John Knopp, Chair, Science Department, Rufus King High School, Milwaukee;
Willette Knopp, Reading Specialist and Elementary Teacher, Fox Point-Bayside (Wis.) School District.

1 2 3 4 5 6 7 8 9 93 92 91 90 89 88

Air is everywhere, but we cannot see it. So how do we know that it really exists? You can feel it if you blow on your hand, and, when the air blows outside, it makes other things move. We call the moving air wind. It can be gentle enough to rustle a few leaves, or strong enough to uproot a whole tree.

It's pretty windy here right now, but the windiest place in the world is in Antarctica, on the coast of Eastern Adélie Land and Western King George Land.

It's hopeless trying to sweep up leaves in this wind!

Winds of up to 216 miles per hour (360 kph) have been recorded. Very strong, fast winds can cause lots of damage.

WOOF!

3

Make your own game of blow soccer!

You need two straws, a ping-pong ball, and two cardboard goals.

You can even catch air if you breathe into a strong paper bag and blow it up. We use air to fill many things, such as footballs, balloons, and bicycle tires. We also use air to help us move around, both on and off the ground.

Potato chip bags are good to blow up, but eat the chips first!

Pop your bag of air with the palm of your hand!

John Dunlop, a Scottish vet, invented the air-filled tire for his son's tricycle.

Did you know that the first bicycles were called "bone shakers?" They had solid tires. Imagine how uncomfortable they must have been to ride!

People have always been excited by the idea of flying through the air. As early as 1010, Eilmer, an Anglo-Saxon monk, built a glider. He flew 200 yards (180 m) in it, crashed, and broke both his legs. He thought that this was because he had not put a tail on the glider.

Around 1480 an Italian engineer invented a parachute, and a few years later Leonardo da Vinci sketched another. Leonardo da Vinci drew many marvelous designs. One was a helicopter, but until the motor was invented it was of no practical use.

A few centuries later came the invention of the hot-air balloon. These balloons were first used in Europe by two Frenchmen, Joseph and Étienne Montgolfier. A hot-air balloon flies because the heated air inside it is lighter than cold air outside.

One of the Montgolfier balloons carried me, Pilâtre de Rozier, and the Marquis d'Arlandes on the world's first aerial journey over Paris on November 21, 1783.

Of course, balloons have their drawbacks. They can only go where the wind takes them!

5

Things that fly in the air have to be both light and strong. Kites are a good example of this. Here is a simple kite that you can make:

You will need 2 balsa wood strips 2ft(½ m) long, and plastic wrap,

a few pieces of tissue paper, an elastic band, and some fishing line.

① Glue wood strips together ⅓ of the way down.

② Loop the elastic band around the crosspiece.

③ Glue the plastic wrap to the wood strips.

④ Glue on the tissue paper tails.

⑤ Tie the fishing line to the crosspiece.

NOW GO FLY YOUR KITE!

Your kite will fly in a very light breeze, but it is not sturdy enough for a really strong wind!

UP

UP

AND

AWAY!

Your kite has wooden struts to support it. Birds also need strong, light supports to help them fly. Because of this their bones are like tubes, with round holes running through the middle. This makes them both light and strong. You can see this if you chop a chicken bone in half — although, of course, chickens can't fly!

FLAP!

WHOOPS!

OU!

Humans have always wanted to fly like birds, but the muscles in their arms are much too weak!

You might have been surprised by what happened. Why is it that the cans move together in the way they do, or that the paper lifts up? The air you blow is moving faster than the air on the outside of the cans. This faster-moving air does not push against the cans as much as the slower-moving air on the outside, so the cans are pushed together inward. Similarly, the sheet of paper is pushed upward by the slower-moving air below it.

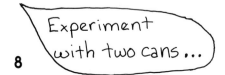

This is called the Bernoulli effect after the Swiss scientist who first discovered it. Try this experiment to find out how the Bernoulli effect is used to help airplanes fly.

Fold a piece of paper like this

Tape edges together

Attach thread to safety pin

Pull the wing quickly across the top of the table — it takes off!

This is why it flies...

FAST-MOVING AIR

AIR

WING

The air has further to go over the top of the wing — so it must move faster!

SLOW-MOVING AIR

WING PUSHED UP

AND NOW FOR A TRICK!

Voilâ! The dog blows the coin!

plate

small coin

The coin leaps onto the plate! The fast-moving air allows it to fly!

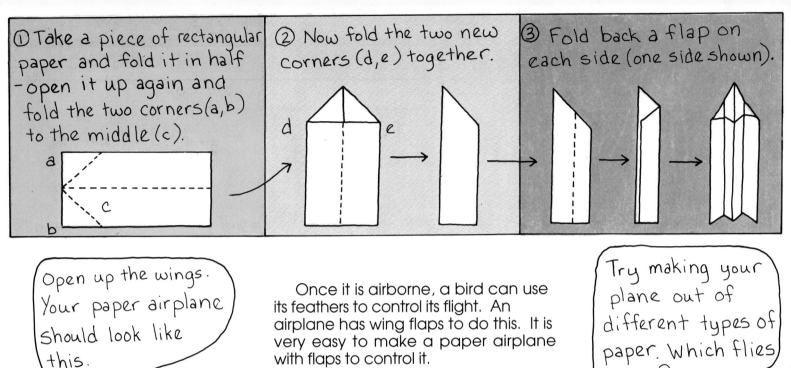

① Take a piece of rectangular paper and fold it in half — open it up again and fold the two corners (a,b) to the middle (c).

② Now fold the two new corners (d,e) together.

③ Fold back a flap on each side (one side shown).

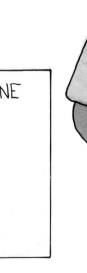

Open up the wings. Your paper airplane should look like this.

Once it is airborne, a bird can use its feathers to control its flight. An airplane has wing flaps to do this. It is very easy to make a paper airplane with flaps to control it.

If you bend one flap slightly down and the other slightly up, the plane will turn to one side when you throw it. With both flaps up it will loop-the-loop. You can experiment to see what else it can do.

Try making your plane out of different types of paper. Which flies best?

WHOOPS!

HOW TO MAKE FLAPS ON YOUR PLANE

fold forward
cut here
cut here
fold forward

10

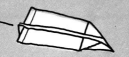

Not all flying-machines have to travel as high as airplanes. Hovercrafts also use air to lift themselves off the ground. You can build your own hovercraft.

You need a plastic margarine tub lid and a cork with a hole through it.

Lid, turned upside down.

Cut hole here.

Glue a cork above hole on lid.

Side View

Attach a balloon over the cork.

Blow up your balloon through the hole.

Then, place your hovercraft on a hard surface.

Now comes the fun part! Whoosh... let your hovercraft go! A gentle tap sends it floating along.

Air rushing out of the balloon under the lid lifts your hovercraft off the ground on a cushion of air.

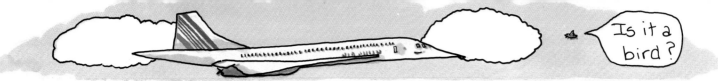

Anything that moves through the air, whether in the sky, on the land, or on the sea, needs to be streamlined. This allows air to flow smoothly over the vehicle and, thereby, helps it to travel faster, using less fuel.

To see how streamlining works, take two pieces of paper and crumple one up. Drop them both. The crumpled one hits the ground first because it is more compact than the flat piece, which flutters slowly down.

The air that surrounds the Earth is called the atmosphere. It is held in place by the Earth's gravity. If our bodies were not strong, this air would squash us. We call this squashing down of the atmosphere air pressure.

In Magdeburg, Germany, in 1657, a scientist called Otto von Guericke set up a strange experiment. He used a special copper ball split in two halves. When these were pushed together, he pumped all the air out of the middle. The air pressure outside held the balls in place. This pressure was so strong that it took 16 horses, eight straining from each side, to pull the balls apart.

MAKE YOUR OWN BAROMETER

① Fill a bottle with water. Hold a bowl over the top of the bottle and quickly turn it upside down.

② Tilt the bottle to allow more air in. Rest two pieces of wood at base of bottle. ⅓ full of air. With tape mark the water levels on both bowl and bottle.

③ Now watch! High air pressure outside will result in the water bottle the level falls (as in the bowl shown). If the pressure is low, opposite the will happen.

Why is air pressure so important to us? Without it we wouldn't be able to drink through a straw, or breathe properly, and suction discs would fall off walls. Our weather would be very different, because it is the changes in air pressure that cause winds and move rain, snow, and warm air around.

Make some weather forecasts with your home-made barometer! Low pressure will indicate that wet, windy, cloudy weather is on the way!

In the summer, high pressure means perfect outdoor weather-hot and dry! But in the winter, it means cold weather.

The highest inhabited area of the world is the Andes. Here people live at a height of 17,700ft (5,400m)!

Because the amount and pressure of air is less, the people here have developed a deep, rapid way of breathing, which results in barrel-like chests!

Some day you might climb a very high mountain, go deep-sea diving, or even take a trip into space! If you do, you will need to take some air with you, since we must have air to breathe.

To find out more about your breathing, try these experiments. Sit down and breathe in and out slowly. Do you feel what happens to your stomach and chest? When you breathe in, your stomach and chest move out to make space for the air to get in.

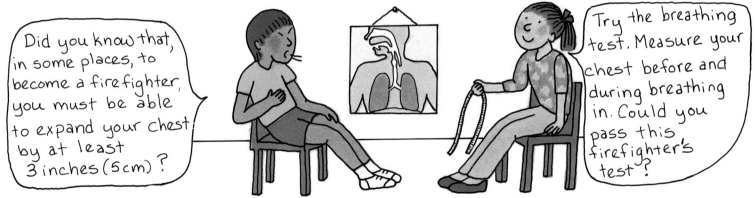

Did you know that, in some places, to become a firefighter, you must be able to expand your chest by at least 3 inches (5cm)?

Try the breathing test. Measure your chest before and during breathing in. Could you pass this firefighter's test?

You will have noticed that you sometimes breathe faster than normal. Sit still and count how many times you breathe in during one minute. Then go for a short run. Now count again how often you breathe in one minute. You will find that you breathe faster in order to get more air into your lungs, so that your body has the energy it needs to run around.

ON YOUR MARK. GET SET, GO!!!

You will find that the candle in the second jar, containing air that you've breathed out, does not stay lit for as long as the candle in the jar containing ordinary air. This is because when you breathe in air, you take a gas called oxygen out of it. The candle needs the oxygen to burn.

This was first discovered about 200 years ago by a French scientist called Lavoisier. He called that part of the air that was needed to make things burn "fire air."

Dragons aren't real. Why am I running? Old stories say that they had huge wings and claws and breathed fire. They must have needed lots of oxygen!

Scientists have also found that as we breathe out, we put another gas called carbon dioxide back into the air. We make carbon dioxide inside our bodies.

Here is a simple way of describing what happens inside us. We need to breathe in oxygen, and we also need to eat food that has lots of a substance called carbon in it. In our bodies the carbon and oxygen join together. When this happens, the energy we need to move around is made. We then have to get rid of the carbon joined to oxygen (carbon dioxide), so we breathe it out.

HOOWWWWWLLLLL

MEOOOWWWWWW

Animals can make awful noises, too!

We can also use air for the everyday business of making a noise! When you talk or shout you are pushing air past cords in your throat. The air vibrates, or shakes, them. You can feel this by putting your fingers against your Adam's apple. The vibrating cords make a noise that you can shape into words, using your mouth and tongue.

Here are some other ways of making a noise with air:

Wrap wax paper around a comb.

Zzzz...

Then blow and hum at the same time.

With a recorder, letting the air escape from different holes makes different noises.

The air box forming part of the guitar or drum makes them sound MUCH LOUDER!

BANG!

Can you play a tune?

TING!

The more air in the bottle, the lower the note when you tap it.

In this way plants keep a balance of oxygen and carbon dioxide in the air. Well, almost a balance. Some scientists think we may be putting too much carbon dioxide into the air by cutting down so many of the world's trees and burning so much wood, coal, and oil. (We will see later that burning fuels produces CO_2.) This could result in what's known as the "greenhouse effect," where the Earth would get much warmer than it is today. The heat from the sun could be trapped in the Earth's atmosphere because of the extra carbon dioxide in the air. It is possible that if it got too warm, the polar ice-caps would start to melt, sea-levels would rise, and low-lying land would be flooded. To avoid this, some scientists think we should stop cutting down and burning so many of the world's forests, especially in South America. Instead we should be planting more trees and using other sources of energy.

Are we destroying our world?

Over the last 100 years the temperature of the atmosphere has risen by about 0.5°F (0.75°c).

Sails are fitted to yachts so that they can be pushed along by the wind.

Air is a possible alternative. We have, in fact, been using air as a source of power for nearly a thousand years. The earliest record of this is in 7th century Iran, where windmills were used to turn millstones for grinding corn. Windmills began to appear in Europe around the 12th century.

Windmills have specially designed sails that spin when the wind blows. These have to be kept facing into the wind. Some windmills have to be turned into the wind by hand, while others have special tail fins to turn them automatically. Most of the early mills were used to grind corn for bread; but in Holland, where areas of land have been reclaimed from the sea, windmills pump water away to prevent flooding. In recent years scientists have been investigating the possibility of using windmills to produce electricity. This may become an important source of energy in the future.

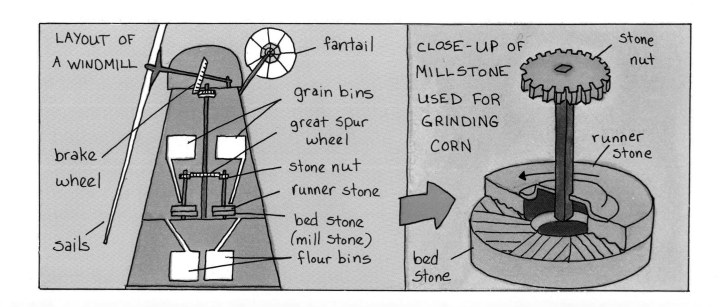

LAYOUT OF A WINDMILL

fantail

grain bins

great spur wheel

stone nut

runner stone

bed stone (mill stone)

flour bins

brake wheel

sails

CLOSE-UP OF MILLSTONE USED FOR GRINDING CORN

stone nut

runner stone

bed stone

21

THE CARBON CYCLE

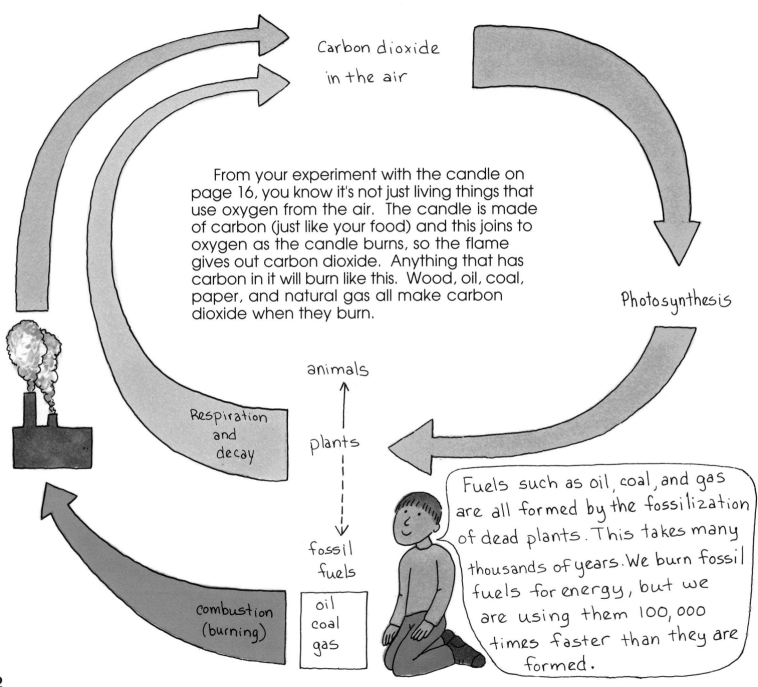

Carbon dioxide in the air

Photosynthesis

From your experiment with the candle on page 16, you know it's not just living things that use oxygen from the air. The candle is made of carbon (just like your food) and this joins to oxygen as the candle burns, so the flame gives out carbon dioxide. Anything that has carbon in it will burn like this. Wood, oil, coal, paper, and natural gas all make carbon dioxide when they burn.

Respiration and decay

animals

plants

fossil fuels

oil
coal
gas

combustion (burning)

Fuels such as oil, coal, and gas are all formed by the fossilization of dead plants. This takes many thousands of years. We burn fossil fuels for energy, but we are using them 100,000 times faster than they are formed.

They also all make soot. You might have noticed a small black mark on the jar above the candle. This is soot, or carbon that didn't burn. Smoke from burning wood and coal has lots of soot in it, and this can pollute the air we breathe. This can be a major problem in some cities unless this burning is banned.

Today people in some big cities must use smokeless fuel for burning in open fires, or use other forms of energy such as gas or electricity.

SMOKELESS FUEL

23

Look at the jar steaming up!

That means the flame must be making water!

You may also have noticed when you did the candle experiment that the inside of your jar steamed up. If you were to wipe it with your finger, it would feel wet. This is because the candle has a substance called hydrogen in it. Like carbon, hydrogen can burn, which means it joins to oxygen. Hydrogen and oxygen joined together make hydrogen oxide. We usually call this water.

H_2O, what's that?

It's hydrogen joined to oxygen. That's how scientists write "water."

H_2OK! Tee-hee!

We need fire (or heat) to produce most of the things we make. But fire can also be very dangerous. To make a fire, three things are needed: oxygen from the air, something that burns (we usually call this a fuel) and heat (this might come from a spark or match). If any one of the three things is removed the fire will go out.

This is the fire triangle.

OXYGEN HEAT FUEL

Never play with fire. If you see younger children playing with matches, stop them!

25

You already know there is oxygen in air. Try this experiment to find out just how much there is. Stick the stub of a candle into the upturned lid of a bottle, and then float this in a bowl of water.

The burning candle uses up the oxygen from the air in the jar. This lets the water rise up inside the jar. Since the water rises about one-fifth of the way up the jar, this suggests that oxygen makes up one-fifth (or 20 %) of the air. Nearly all of the remaining four-fifths of the air is made up of a gas called nitrogen. There are other gases as well. You know about carbon dioxide and water, because you breathe them out. Air also contains a small amount of five other gases: helium, neon, argon, krypton, and xenon.

Oxygen is very important in space technology! Without it, humans could never have gone to the moon!

We use very cold liquid oxygen to fire the rockets, and we must take a supply of oxygen (mixed with nitrogen) so we can breathe in space. We can even cut steel in space with the help of oxygen mixed with acetylene. This produces a very hot flame, 5432°F (3000°C)!

LIQUID HYDROGEN

LIQUID OXYGEN

All of these gases can be useful.

Oxygen, as we have seen, is essential to us. It is used in hospitals for people with breathing difficulties, but it also has many other uses, such as for making steel.

Carbon dioxide puts the fizz in fizzy drinks. These are the bubbles you see when you open a bottle or can. Rock music groups sometimes use cold, solid lumps of carbon dioxide, known as "dry ice," on stage. As this melts, it sends white clouds across the stage like fog. The gas stays low, because it is heavier than air.

Carbon dioxide is very important in bread-making. Why? Well, without it the bread is flat and quite hard. We call this unleavened bread.

To make bread dough, you mix flour and water. You add a small amount of sugar and yeast, a type of fungus. You then leave the dough in a warm place for an hour or two. The yeast cells multiply and give off CO_2, and the dough rises. When the dough is baked in a hot oven, the heat kills the yeast and bakes the bread!

Nitrogen occurs naturally in manure.

They don't call me Nitrogen Ned for nothing!

Nitrogen is used in making fertilizers, explosives, dyes, and many drugs. You may have seen large tank trucks with signs saying "Liquid Nitrogen." This is the way it is often transported. Nitrogen must be very cold to turn into a liquid. Nitrogen turns from a gas to a liquid at 320° F below zero (-196° C).

One way to make your own fertilizer is to build a compost heap!

When your compost is ready, put it on the soil surrounding your plants. The nitrogen in the decayed matter is absorbed by the plants, making them grow much better.

What you'll need is a container with a rainproof lid. Add lots of rotting vegetable matter, such as potato peelings and old cabbages. Add layers of fertilizers and lime occasionally! Shelter your compost heap from the sun and the wind, turn it over now and again, and keep it moist!

lid

vegetable matter

vegetable matter

vegetable matter

vegetable matter

container

brick

grill allows air to get to compost

Helium, a very light gas, is used in weather balloons. It can also be used in larger airships, called blimps, which can carry many people. Hydrogen used to be used in blimps, but it burns very easily and led to a number of terrible disasters in which many people were killed. The most notorious was the crash of the airship Hindenberg in 1937.

29

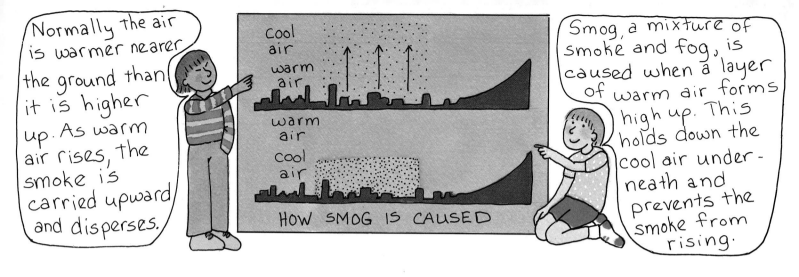

Normally the air is warmer nearer the ground than it is higher up. As warm air rises, the smoke is carried upward and disperses.

Smog, a mixture of smoke and fog, is caused when a layer of warm air forms high up. This holds down the cool air underneath and prevents the smoke from rising.

Cool air
warm air

warm air
cool air

HOW SMOG IS CAUSED

We are also constantly polluting our air by putting gases into it that shouldn't be there. Exhaust fumes from cars, for example, contain both carbon monoxide, which is a poisonous gas, and an acid gas called nitric oxide. This acid gas, which is also produced in large amounts by factories, attacks plants and metals, and causes bricks on buildings to crumble. It dissolves in rain, making acid rain, which has been responsible for destroying trees and killing animals in lakes in parts of North America and Northern Europe. Car fumes also contain lead. This is a poisonous metal and can be very dangerous to young children.

WHAT'S IN CIGARETTE SMOKE

CARBON MONOXIDE - the poisonous car exhaust gas.

HYDROGEN CYANIDE - a poisonous gas.

Get the message? Don't smoke cigarettes. They pollute our air and our lungs!

AMMONIA - used in oven cleaners.

NITROGEN DIOXIDE - forms an acid in water. We have water in our lungs!

What's that?

That's lichen. It grows all over tree bark when the air is clean and unpolluted.

It's a cat, of course!

WOOF!

BAAA!

The problem of air pollution is a very serious one, but steps can be taken to improve the situation. Lead is being banned from fuel in North America and may soon be banned throughout Europe. New controls are being developed to stop factories from producing nitric oxide. More work is being done and must be done to clean up the mess we make of our air. The air is very important to us. We all share it and we must take care of it.

Plants grow much better in clean air. They taste better, too!

Glossary

Air: space above the Earth; an invisible mixture of gases — 78% nitrogen, 21% oxgyen, 1% other gases.

Atmosphere: the air that surrounds the Earth, extending 22,000 miles (35,398 km) and rotating with the Earth.

Barometer: an instrument that measures the pressure of the Earth's atmosphere, making it possible to predict weather.

Carbon dioxide: the gas that passes out of our lungs when we breathe; also used in fire extinguishers and soft drinks.

Carbon monoxide: a poisonous gas produced most commonly by gasoline-burning cars and by smoking materials such as pipes, cigars, and cigarettes.

Fossilization: the process of turning formerly living material into another form, usually rock, over a long time.

Gravity: the force that draws all objects in the Earth's sphere toward the Earth's center.

Greenhouse effect: the gradual rise in the Earth's temperature.

Helium: a gaseous element used to inflate and lift balloons.

Oxygen: the gas that is essential for all life processes and for fire to burn; it is produced by plants.

Photosynthesis: the process by which plants make food from carbon dioxide in sunlight and release oxygen into the air.

Streamlined: having a shape that makes moving through air or water easy; usually narrow in front with few parts sticking out.

Wind: moving air.

Index